TECH TRACK™

BUILDING YOUR CAREER IN IT

BECOMING A SOFTWARE ENGINEER

AMIE JANE LEAVITT

Rosen YA™

New York

Published in 2018 by The Rosen Publishing Group, Inc.
29 East 21st Street, New York, NY 10010

First Edition

Library of Congress Cataloging-in-Publication Data

Names: Leavitt, Amie Jane, author.
Title: Becoming a software engineer / Amie Jane Leavitt.
Description: New York, NY : Rosen Publishing, 2018. | Series: Tech track: building your career in IT | Audience: Grades 7–12. | Includes bibliographical references and index.
Identifiers: LCCN 2017001586 | ISBN 9781508175544 (library bound book)
Subjects: LCSH: Software engineering—Vocational guidance—Juvenile literature. | Computer scientists—Juvenile literature.
Classification: LCC QA76.758 .L43 2018 | DDC 005.1092—dc23
LC record available at https://lccn.loc.gov/2017001586

Manufactured in the United States of America

Contents

INTRODUCTION

After cycling to work on a sunny Monday morning, Julia—a software engineer at a major internet company in the Bay Area—grabs breakfast from the company cafeteria and heads down the hall to the computing room. Here, she meets with other software engineers and the project manager for their daily standup meeting. During this brief get-together, the team discusses their current project. Team members report on their progress, brainstorm suggestions for any development issues, and set goals for the workday.

Following the meeting, Julia makes her way to her desk, sits down on her ergonomic chair in front of her ergonomic keyboard and two large monitors, and gets to work. The monitors provide Julia with plenty of screen space so she doesn't have to toggle back and forth between the various programs and pages she may be utilizing during the workday. This setup is crucial for anyone who spends large amounts of time on their computers. It drastically increases their productivity.

For the first half-hour that Julia spends at her desk, she generally reads and responds to emails, focusing on the most important ones first. Emails can be a real time drain, so Julia tries to spend only a small amount of time on this task in the morning and then revisit her inbox in the afternoon.

Since office workers generally spend large amounts of time at their desks, ergonomic workstations are imperative.

As a software engineer, Julia needs to spend the bulk of her day writing and testing code. She works with a variety of coding languages during the day, depending on what type of project she is working on. All of the back-end systems of her projects are in Python and the front-end systems are in JavaScript, HTML, and CSS. During the day, Julia frequently moves back and forth between the languages to address different issues and create coding for her projects. Since Julia and her team members are seated near each other, if any of them run into problems as they work, they can just stand up and ask the other members for suggestions. Julia usually asks and answers many questions throughout the day.

At noon, Julia desperately needs to get out of her chair and move, since she has been working nonstop at her desk since 9:30 a.m.. She is lucky enough to work for a big corporation that has a lot of amenities for its employees, such as rock climbing walls, fitness rooms, and even a bowling alley. She decides to spend half an hour scaling the rock climbing wall and then grab a quick lunch at the cafeteria before she heads back to her desk to continue with her projects.

Afternoons for Julia are generally split between coding, meetings, and emails. Today, Julia catches up on her emails as soon as she gets back from lunch and then spends an hour in a meeting about a new project the company hopes to start the following month. After the meeting, Julia returns to her desk and spends the next several hours coding. She is anxious to finish up one area of her project so she can test for workability. She sets herself a goal of 5 p.m. to finish, and happily, achieves it. Julia tests the web page to make sure it works as she intends and unfortunately discovers some bugs. Julia asks a few of her colleagues for recommendations and makes notes of what she needs to try out tomorrow morning.

Big software companies like Google provide amenities for their employees, including rock walls. This helps boost morale and increase overall happiness and performance at work.

At about 5 p.m., Julia notices some of her team members leaving for the day and decides she also needs to follow suit. While she could just keep working throughout the night to resolve the bugs, Julia knows she needs to have a balance in her life if she wants to be a good programmer. There will always be more work to complete tomorrow! Julia closes down her workstation, grabs her cycle from the bike rack, and pedals back home, where she spends the evening relaxing with friends.

CHAPTER ONE

WHAT IS IT?

As a software engineer, Julia works in the world of IT, or information technology. The term "information technology" is defined as "the study or use of systems for retrieving, storing, and sending information." In information technology, those systems are computers and telecommunication devices. Information technology includes all parts of these systems: the hardware or physical machines and components, the software or programs that run the hardware, the networks or connections between the machines, and the internet or global connections of computer networks.

THE FATHER OF THE COMPUTER

The history of computers, surprisingly, stretches all the way back to the year 1822. A man named Charles Babbage—a British mathematician, inventor, and mechanical

Charles Babbage invented the first computing machine, or computer, in England in 1822.

engineer—came up with the idea for the first mechanical computer. Babbage lived during the time of the Industrial Revolution, a time when machines automated many tasks originally performed by humans and animals. Everything relied heavily on numbers and calculations which were performed by mathematicians and then recorded on numerical tables. If a calculation was off, or if a person had made an error in transcribing numbers onto the table, there could be disastrous consequences: ships could run aground if navigational tables were even a hundredth of a point off, bridges could fail if measurements were incorrectly calculated, and so forth. As a mathematician, Babbage worried about the errors that he and his associates could accidentally make and the problems that could result. As an inventor, he set out to build a machine that would be able to calculate error-free numerical tables.

Babbage's idea, which was obviously hugely revolutionary for the time, was for a steam-driven calculating machine that would use a series of rotating gears to complete complex polynomial equations. It would be called the Difference Engine because it could only complete addition—it could not multiply and divide. Babbage sketched detailed drawings, received funding from the British government, and found a toolmaker to construct it.

His mammoth machine called for 25,000 unique parts. At that time, specialization had not yet been invented—which meant he couldn't just run down and buy a bolt at the tool store and know that it would have worked on his project. Every single part, down to those nuts and bolts, had to be crafted specifically for that one machine. Unsurprisingly, problems arose and only a portion of the machine was built.

Years later, in 1847, Babbage streamlined his design (cutting down the parts needed to only 8,000) and named the improved machine the Difference Engine II. However, this time, Babbage's ideas never even left his notebooks. The machine sadly was never built during Babbage's lifetime. In 1985, the Science Museum of London finally decided to construct his machine. It took seventeen years to complete the machine, which stood seven feet high, eleven feet long, and weighed five tons! It worked just as Babbage had hoped it would.

Today, Babbage is known as the "father of the computer." However, it was actually a different machine that

A model of Babbage's Analytical Engine is owned by the National Museum of Science and Industry in London.

Babbage created in between the Difference Engines I and II that gave him that title. This invention was called the Analytical Engine, and Babbage conceived of it in 1834.

This machine would be fully programmable and able to perform any type of calculation. It would be made up of four components: mill, store, reader, and printer. The "mill" would be the calculating part of the machine (similar to a CPU unit in a modern computer). The "store" would be where data was held before it was processed (similar to memory in a modern computer). Babbage's store would be able to hold 1,000 50-digit numbers. The "reader" would be the input device for the machine. Input devices on a modern computer are the keyboard, mouse, digital scanner, and so forth—anything that allows the user to enter information into the computer.

On Babbage's machine, he planned to use punch cards to enter data and other information into the computer. The punch card idea had been invented by a French man named Joseph-Marie Jacquard on his textile manufacturing machine in 1801. By using punch cards, Babbage could program his machine and thereby make it flexible, or changeable. This characteristic of flexibility is an essential principle used in modern computers and is achieved through software engineering.

Finally, the machine would have three outputs: a printer (which would print numbers on rolled paper), a curve plotter (which would print graphics), and a bell that would alert the operator to do certain tasks (change a punch card, fix an error, and so forth). All of these ideas were beyond remarkable considering this was the early 1800s! Unfortunately, as is true with all of Babbage's other machines, the Analytical Engine was never built. If it had, it truly would have been 100 years ahead of its time!

Interview with a Software Engineer: Casey Allred

Describe your experience working as a software engineer.

Every day is both similar and completely different at the same time. Similar in the sense that I'm using the same tools and working on the same code, but different in that rarely is any problem the exact same as the one before. I love coming into work knowing that there will probably be a challenge that pops up that will require me to think and often to dive deeper in understanding how the program works in order to solve it. Often that requires me to work with the team and even other non-programmers to really get at the root of the problem and fix it. In short, you get to work with highly skilled people and awesome technology to build amazing products.

Why did you choose this particular profession, and how did you get your education/training?

I sort of evolved into being a computer scientist when my dad brought home a computer when I was around the age of eight. I enjoyed playing games, and during the winter it was a great way to have fun after we were too cold to stay outside. When my dad brought home another computer, I attempted to install a modem and ended up frying the whole thing. That's when my true love of computers was born! For the longest time I thought I was going to build robots or do something in hardware, but as I got into school I constantly drifted towards programming because not only was it cheaper, but I could see the results of my work much quicker. Also while I was in college, I got a job doing web development... I then used that skill to pay my way through college, and it led to me enjoying the job I have today. Most of the technical skills I use every day I have taught myself, but college gave me a deeper understanding and aided me in developing those skills to a much higher level than if I had chosen not to go.

20TH-CENTURY COMPUTERS

Just like Babbage's machines, early-20th-century computers were all enormous in size. Colossus, which is considered the first electronic computer, for example, was constructed during World War II. It was seven feet high (2.13 meters), 17 ft wide (5.18 m), and 11 ft deep (3.35 m). It weighed five tons (4.54 metric tons), used 2,500 vacuum tubes or valves, 100 logic gates, and 10,000 resistors and 4,349 miles (7,000 kilometers) of wires. SAGE, the world's largest computer ever built, was constructed in 1957 by IBM. It just didn't fill a room; it stretched across 20 different locations called Direction Centers (DC), with the computers in each being about an acre in size! Every DC, a building built like a cube, had two central processing units (CPUs) in them. Each CPU

Women from the Women's Royal Naval Service (nicknamed "Wrens") operate a Colossus Mark II. This British computer helped crack Hitler's code, aiding the Allies' victory in World War II.

covered 7,500 square feet (696.77 square meters) of space, had 60,000 vacuum tubes, 175,000 diodes, 13,000 transistors, a 256KB of magnetic core RAM, and weighed 250 tons (226.8 metric tons). Each CPU could perform 75,000 instructions per second.

The jobs of these early computers were essentially to solve big data problems. Colossus was built to crack Adolf Hitler's Enigma code. Colossus worked around the clock, crunching numbers at superhuman speeds, in an effort to decipher coded messages sent by Hitler to his generals. The Nazis used a machine called Enigma that could scramble a message in an infinite number of ways, and each day the code would be changed. There was no way a person could manually run through all of the various combinations in order to crack the daily codes, but Colossus could. Colossus, therefore, is credited with shortening the war and saving millions of lives.

SAGE was used to crunch numbers during the Cold War. During this time, radar installations throughout North America were gathering information on Soviet missiles and bombers. This produced a vast amount of data that needed to be analyzed immediately. SAGE, with its number-crunching technology, was able to help the United States attain the information it needed to keep the country safe from possible attacks. Other similar computers, which were developed during the 1950s and '60s, helped advance science, business, and medicine—and were even used by NASA to send a man to the moon.

What Overall Skills, Traits, and Personalities Are Needed for Software Engineering?

Many different types of people are attracted to the career of software engineering. However, they do have some traits in common. Here are three of them:

1. **Adaptability.** Software engineers need to be adaptable in a variety of contexts. First of all, the nature of their work is constantly changing, so they need to be able to roll with problems when they arise and be willing to take the time to fix them. Second, software engineers often have dual roles throughout their workday. Generally, software engineers are members of a team where everyone is working on the same project together. So, a willingness to help others on the team and get help from others is necessary. Throughout the day, software engineers often work individually on their own part of the project. Since this requires hours and hours of alone time staring at a computer screen, software engineers must also be good independent workers, too. The back-and-forth of switching between teamwork and individual work during the average workday makes the trait of adaptability very helpful for software engineers.
2. **Creativity.** Software engineers are creating new projects all the time. While they do this in a technical way, they must also maintain a vision of what the final product will be like. Video game and app designers have a great amount of creativity to be successful at their jobs.

3. **Problem Solving.** Software engineers must enjoy solving problems. Software engineer Roy Hayward says, "If you get frustrated installing a printer or figuring out why you can't attach a photo to an email, you might not want to pursue a career where you are trying to build an algorithm that will take weeks to get working right." Software engineers can spend hours and days working the bugs out of a program or trying to make an app behave in a certain way. So along with the ability to problem-solve, software engineers also must have a great amount of patience in order to make it through the trial-and-error process that this type of career often requires.

AN EXCITING PAST AND FUTURE

Of course, the full history of computers and information technology cannot possibly be covered in just a few sections of a book. These tidbits of historical facts have been provided as a way to illustrate just how far information technology has come in a relatively short period of time, and to get you excited about the types of technological advances that could be in store for us in the future. The world of information technology is truly a fascinating one:

there are technological advancements and innovations on this planet being made every single second of every single day. And the best part about all of this is that information technology is truly open to anyone, anywhere. It's open to you! All you need to have is the desire to learn, the freedom to dream, and the skills and tools to make your dreams a reality.

There are countless ways that people can make an impact in information technology. Many IT professionals work in such areas as systems analysis, network administration, web development, technical support, and so forth. People are also needed to design and build the machines: the "hardware," or physical components of the computers. These hardware engineers build the sensors and circuit boards and design operating systems. They are also the people, for example, who figure out what the next smartphones will look like. They determine what type of material the phone will be made out of, the type of battery that will power it, and the type of processor that will run it.

Other IT professionals, called software engineers, design the "software," or programs, that run the machines. Originally, as was described previously in Babbage's Analytical Engine, these programs were coded onto thousands of punch cards and entered physically into the computer or, in later machines, stored on magnetic tapes or discs. Today, the codes are written by software engineers and then stored in the system's memory. Software is incredibly important to the operation of a computer. Without it, your

This small smartphone has immensely more capabilities than any of the room-sized machines that existed in the early days of computers. But without software, it is useless.

smartphone would essentially be a useless paperweight made of plastic and glass. It would not be capable of doing anything if the software in its memory wasn't telling it to do so.

Since this book is specifically about what it takes to become a software engineer, the subsequent chapters of this book will deal with this particular area of IT in greater detail. Other books in this series will deal with some of the other jobs available in the exciting world of information technology.

CHAPTER TWO

WHAT OPPORTUNITIES ARE AVAILABLE TO A SOFTWARE ENGINEER?

A software engineer is an IT professional who creates, designs, writes, and tests the programs used by computers and the internet. Software engineers work in all kinds of industries. Some, like Laureen A. Ervin, work in the aerospace industry. When she worked at the Boeing Company, for example, she wrote software for airplane flight simulators. Prior to her work in aerospace, Ervin worked in the medical equipment industry, writing software for hospital equipment such as electrocardiograms (ECGs) and ultrasound machines. Software engineer Chris Rapposelli-Manzo worked for the government and telecommunications companies during her career. Her government contracts included writing software for military aircraft and mail-sorting equipment. For the telecomm companies, she wrote software for data communications equipment. Software engineer Moriya Chesler used her software engineering skills to pursue her entrepreneurial ambitions. She started her own company, where she produces digital sewing patterns for modest clothing using her own pattern-making software.

A Sampling of Subfields in Software Engineering

Just like software engineers can work in a variety of industries, they also can work in many different capacities. There are many different ways that the skills of software engineering can be utilized in the 21st century job market. The listings below are a sample of some of the opportunities available to software engineers—keep in mind, there are many more types available.

Front-End Developers

These engineers work with the code that runs the part of a website that a user interacts with, which is called the client-side. These developers work primarily with the back-end developers (see description below) and designers who give them a mock-up of the website that needs to be built. Front-end engineers work with HTML code to establish the general structure of the site; CSS code to make the site beautiful through the use of various colors, font styles, spacing, and padding; and then JavaScript to make the website interactive through buttons, links, and so forth.

Gareth Ballester is a senior front-end engineer for an automotive industry website. He started out as a web designer and got more into the coding end of things over time. Ballester explains that as a front-end designer, a developer must be able to work with design elements, be concerned with the experience of the user, and ensure that the data can be incorporated on the back end.

His favorite part of front-end developing is that he gets to solve interesting problems: "I get a mock-up of how something should look and how it should work, and I have to figure out how to make that happen. There's lots

Front-end developers, such as this woman, present their ideas to clients and listen to their feedback. They are responsible for the face of the website, with which users see and interact.

of different challenges around that, so it's rewarding to figure those all out and then in the end you have something you can touch and use and click on."

Back-End Developers

These engineers work with the code and algorithms that run the behind-the-scenes or foundation part of a website, called the server-side. There are three parts of the server-side: the server, the database, and the server-side applications. The back-end is truly the brain of the website.

Some like to think of a back-end developer this way: if building a website is like building a house, then the back-end workers are the people who dig the foundation, pour the concrete, build the framework, and insert the necessary plumbing and wiring into the structure. These are all parts of the house that people don't directly use, but they are necessary for the structure of the home. The front-end developers are the people who install the components of the house that the person will directly use, like the faucets and the light switches. Back-end developers work closely with front-end developers, since the two parts of the website must work together for it to function properly. Back-end people have knowledge of general programming languages (PHP, Java, C#, Ruby, Python, JavaScript, and so forth). They also have database expertise and knowledge of web services.

Interview with a Software Engineer: Roy Hayward

Why did you decide to become a software engineer, and what path did you take to get to the position you are in today?

I wasn't planning to be a programmer or software engineer. I started out studying chemistry in college. Then I switched to political science. When I got out of college and got a job, I was way more interested in the computers we were using than the job we were doing with them. So I quit and got into computer tech support. I worked my way up to a programming job from there. It took me about three years before I landed my first programming job. After that, I knew I had found the place for me.

What are the pros/cons of this career?

For me, the biggest pro for this career is that computers were always my hobby. So I get paid to do something that I would want to do even if I wasn't getting paid. Another pro in this business is the ability to work from a variety of locations. I've had telecommuting jobs and been able to dial in and work while traveling. This adds to the job's flexibility.

Interestingly, the job's flexibility is also the biggest con of the career. I've had jobs where I got called at 2 a.m. or on Christmas when something stopped working and I had to fix it.

What can teens interested in this career do NOW to prepare for a career as a software engineer?

The two biggest things that helped me to be a

programmer today was that I started programming when I was a kid. And today programming is even easier. If I were a kid today, I'd get a website and write code for it. I'd also play with mobile app development. There are plenty of free-to-cheap ways to start coding. Specific languages aren't as important as developing the skill of solving problems and doing tasks by giving the computer instructions to do it for you. So using a free language and platform is where I would start.

Mobile Engineers

These engineers create a variety of software types that are specifically designed for mobile devices (smartphones, tablets, and so forth). The mobile environment is different from the desktop environment, and because of that, device-specific software has to be designed to suit the mobile platform.

One example of this is websites. Websites are not going to look the same on a computer and mobile device. A website that was designed primarily for a desktop computer will need to be adapted to allow a mobile user to pinch or zoom the screen in order to interact with it. To solve this problem, mobile engineers design software that permits websites to be more friendly for the user:

menu screens are reconfigured, larger navigation buttons are used, images are increased in size, and content is reformatted. Another task that mobile engineers work on is voice recognition or multi-application voice processing. Many people utilize the microphone on their mobile devices for more than just talking on the phone—they conduct searches on web browsers, tell their device to make a call or search for a phone number, and even write texts by speaking into the phone and having the device translate the spoken words into text. All of these tasks are only possible because a mobile software engineer created a program that tells the mobile device how to do them. Mobile engineers work in Android and iOS platforms and generally have knowledge of Java, Objective-C, and C++.

Application (App) Developers

An app is any computer program that is used by a consumer to complete a specific task. Word processing programs are an example of apps. So are media players, calculators, web browsers, spreadsheets, slide presentations, photo editing programs, and even battlefield and airplane flight simulators. There are also apps designed specifically for mobile devices. These are called mobile apps.

Scroll through the apps on your smartphone. Every one of these programs was created by an app developer. App development starts out with a need: "I sure would like to know which gas station has the best price for gas

Applications (apps) allow mobile devices to perform specific functions. These apps are created by software engineers.

in my area." Once the need has been established, an app developer begins brainstorming ways to solve the problem with a mobile app. App developers can't actually create an app, however, without having some basic technical knowledge. For starters, they need to know Objective-C for the iOS platform and Java for Android. Time is also something of great value for an app developer, since most basic apps (v1.0) will generally take between four to six months to build. Grant Goodman, an iOS app developer since age 15, confirmed this in an article in *US News & World Report*, saying that it takes consistent effort for about four or five months to build even the most basic apps.

GAME DEVELOPERS

These engineers develop the software that runs video games. Game developers create games that can be played on consoles or mobile devices. They work closely with designers who have ideas for games and then build the codes that make the games work. Generally, the people who are happiest building this type of software are people who enjoy playing video games, have some kind of art or creative background, and can work with a variety of people (artists, designers, and technical experts). Game

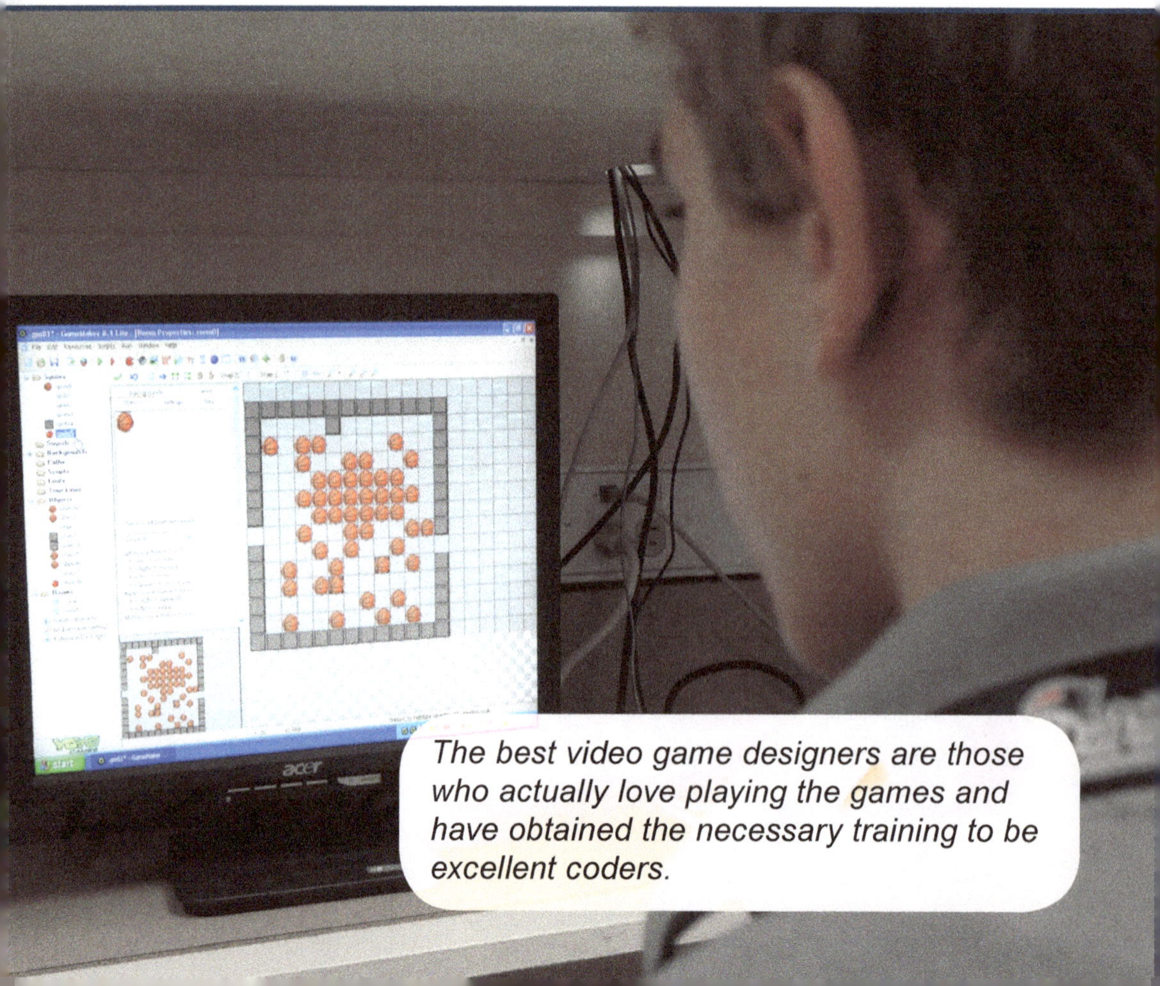

The best video game designers are those who actually love playing the games and have obtained the necessary training to be excellent coders.

developer Joshua McGrath explains, "A strong background in computer science, algorithm-driven, is important [for gaming] because it gives a logical foundation. It's very difficult to substitute a good computer science education." Because game developers are gamers themselves, they know and understand how the games work and what makes a good game. It's important to note that most of a developer's time on the job is not spent playing video games, but rather writing code and working with spreadsheets and databases.

QA/Testing

Once a software program is written, it has to be tested to see if it will work as intended. If it doesn't, the engineers who wrote it need to go back into the program and figure out how to fix the bugs. The best way to test the programs is to design software that will run through the program to find any issues. Sayari Ghosh is a software test analyst. Her job is to write software that tests other programs. She explained the importance of her job in an interview on Engineergirl.org. "Manually testing software is time-consuming, tedious, and an error-prone process," she says. "My work is to figure out which tests can be automated and then write programs that will tell us if something is wrong." Many skills are necessary for software engineers who work in QA/Testing. They need to have good communication skills so they can explain the type of testing they plan on doing with the rest of the development team. They need the ability to think outside the box because many potential problems with software may not be obvious, surface-level ones. They also need advanced technical and analytical skills in order to know what types of problems could arise with software and how to develop software to test for those problems.

Projected Growth Rate for Software Engineering

According to the US Department of Labor's Bureau of Labor Statistics (BLS), jobs in the area of software engineering (or software development) are expected to grow substantially between 2014 and 2024. Here's the breakdown:

Overall, for software developers, the average growth rate is expected to be 17 percent. This breaks down into the following percentages based on specific software engineer niches. For software developers who specialize in applications (apps), the growth rate is expected to be 19 percent. For software developers who develop systems software, the growth rate is expected to be 13 percent. All computer occupations in general are expected to have a 12 percent growth rate during this time period.

These expected growth rates are impressive considering that average growth for all other occupations in the US job market over this same ten-year period is only 7 percent! Think about that: for some of these jobs, their expected growth rate is about double the national average.

With the advent of smartphones and other similar devices, the need for apps has grown tremendously over the past several years. That need will only continue to grow as more smart technology is created, which is reflected by the projected growth rate of 19 percent. A common phrase that people often express when they have something that needs to be solved by technology is, "There's an app for that." The idea behind this phrase is that if there isn't an app for something already, then there's a good chance it can be developed by someone, somewhere, and maybe even by you! App developing is big business, both now and in the future.

Systems developers are finding a lot of opportunities with the Internet of Things wave that is spreading around the globe. According to recent technology trends, more home devices, appliances, and other consumer products will have built-in technology that will link them with each other and with smart devices to be operated remotely. The technology to run these devices will be developed by none other than systems developers. Because of that, the growth rate for jobs in this sector is expected to be 13 percent.

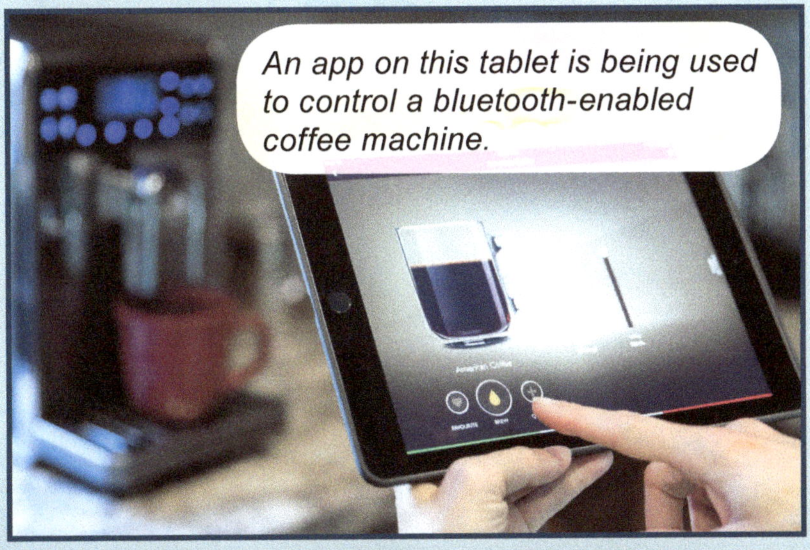

An app on this tablet is being used to control a bluetooth-enabled coffee machine.

MANY OTHER ROLES

In addition to the aforementioned subfields, there are numerous others currently needed on the market, and many others that will be invented as the field of information technology continues to advance. Other subfields that are part of software engineering include embedded systems developers, operating systems (OS) developers, full-stack engineers, language compilers, Dev-Ops (also known as network or system administrators), data scientists, cloud computing engineers, and software security developers.

CHAPTER THREE

Getting the Skills

Most jobs in software engineering require a blend of formal education and relevant experience. On the topic of education, software engineer Paul DeVe says, "In the earlier days, it was possible to get a software engineering job without any sort of college degree. There were so many jobs available and the technology was so new that all it took was proving that you had a little skill and you'd get hired." But things are different these days: "Now that everything is more established, a college degree is a necessity. Getting a bachelor's degree in computer science will help get you in the door, and the connections that universities have to local companies will help immensely with internships and eventual permanent positions." Students with associate degrees in software engineering generally find more entry-level positions, such as computer support specialists and technicians. This is also a good starting point to eventually return to school to complete more education. Most of the higher-paying jobs require applicants to have a bachelor's or master's degree. To be a software engineer, students should focus their study on one of the following majors: computer science, software engineering, or computer information systems.

COLLEGE BOUND

Computer science-related degrees will generally cover such topics as foundations of computing, programming languages, data management, software design, systems programming, data structure and algorithms, database systems, operating systems, mobile design, and so forth. Some of these classes, like programming languages, will

Software engineers generally work on teams to complete a common project. These teams may operate in the same office space, or they can work remotely and collaborate via the web.

require individualized coursework. Yet, others will require collaborative work. Since software engineers generally work together with members of a team in the workforce, getting this experience in college helps a student become comfortable with working in big teams.

A student named Shawn at the University of West Florida was interviewed about his experience as a software engineering student. He explained that in one of his classes, he and his team worked with a client over a semester to develop software to solve a specific need, which, as he said, was "a challenge but very rewarding in the end." He explained that "one of the most challenging parts of a degree in software engineering is learning the languages and applying them to formulate big algorithms and solve problems." Students, he explained, also need to be prepared to take advanced math through Calculus II. At the end of a degree in software engineering, students are often required to complete a capstone project. This big final project showcases all the key skills that the students have learned though their educational experiences thus far.

Choosing a school can be a challenging venture for anyone. The sidebar on page 59 lists the top ten schools for computer engineering in the United States. Research these programs online and find out what they have to offer. What makes them so special? Are the programs at these schools what will really help you get the type of career you want, or would another school suffice? You may decide to attend one of these top schools, but you also may not. College students are encouraged to do research to find the best school (location, price, and program) that suits their individual needs. Don't think that attending a top school is necessary in order to be marketable in the industry. There are many other colleges and universities throughout the country that offer degrees in computer engineering. The following questions will help you evaluate a program and see if it will help you get the education you need to succeed:

- Does the school provide a variety of research opportunities?
- Do the classes offer opportunities for collaborative, real-world experiences?
- Does the school have a good relationship with companies where students can complete internships?
- What types of awards, scholarships, and fellowships does the school regularly give out?

Online schools are also a way to attain a degree in software engineering, and they offer tremendous opportunities for students. First, they give people who do not live near a university a chance to further their education. Second, they allow working adults the opportunity to get a degree on the evenings and weekends without having to quit their day job. Third, they allow teens to take college-level classes while they are still in high school. Fourth, they allow students a chance to collaborate with other students who may live all over the world. Software engineering is a global industry, and so the more multicultural experience an engineer can get, the more marketable they will be in the workforce.

Relevant experience can be attained through your own initiative on your own computer. Take an online course, design a website, or learn to code from home.

INDIVIDUAL INITIATIVE

To most companies, relevant experience these days is equally as important as formal education. Yet, many job seekers argue, How am I supposed to get experience if I can't get a job? This mindset may work for other types of occupations where experience can only be attained through actual employment, but it certainly does not pertain to software engineering.

Essentially, anyone with an interest in software engineering can get ample experience to put on their résumé through their own initiative. One developer explained that the PCs used by the everyday person are just as good (and usually exactly the same!) as the ones used by the pros in the field. Therefore, anyone with an interest in software engineering can build websites, learn coding, design a video game, or build an app.

They can also get experience working with a team by taking part in hackathons. Experts recommend that budding software engineers should participate in as many of these types of events as they can.

It's this type of relevant experience that shows companies an applicant's true passion for software engineering. Sam Schillace, a senior vice president of engineering at Box, was interviewed by *US News & World Report* on this topic. He explains, "We look at track records as much as school—someone from a great school with no outside coding projects or interesting technical accomplishments is definitely less interesting, and someone who is a rock star coder with no degree but a huge list of achievements would be an easy hire."

Dive in Now

Many software engineers recommend taking advantage of the variety of programs available online (some of which are free) in order to learn how to code. Codecademy is one of those free online schools and was listed in *PC Magazine*'s "Best Programs to Learn to Code for 2016." One of the success stories on Codecademy's website is of a pair of homeschooled teens from Texas who learned

Hackathons

According to *Merriam-Webster,* a term that ends with the suffix -athon is generally an event that lasts a long time or involves a lot of something. For example, a marathon is a super-long running event; a readathon is an event where people read for hours on end; a walkathon or jumpathon are events where people walk or jump rope for a certain distance or certain length of time in order to earn money for a cause.

With that definition in mind, a hackathon is an event that lasts a specific amount of time, generally one or two days or over a weekend. This event is where computer programmers assemble with the purpose of working together to design IT that solves real-world problems. The end result can be anything from an app, a website, game, or even a robot.

At hackathons, computer programmers are placed in groups with strangers. The teams collaborate, brainstorm ideas, and come up with a plan to solve a specific problem that they've been given. During the length of the hackathon, the teams will work as quickly as possible to complete their task. Just like no one takes a nap during a marathon, no one sleeps during a hackathon either. The teams are working against the clock to finish up their project before the time is up. At the end of the hackathon, the teams showcase their final products, and a winner is chosen and awarded with prizes.

Over the years, some very successful products have resulted from hackathons. In 2010, a team created a product that eventually became the GroupMe app. This app was later sold to Skype for $85 million! The "like" button on Facebook was also the result of a hackathon, except it was one that Facebook promoted with its own employees. Brilliantly, both

SIDEBAR CONTINUED ON THE NEXT PAGE

SIDEBAR CONTINUED FROM THE PREVIOUS PAGE

These women are hard at work during the "Tech for Good" ethical hackathon, part of the Grace Hopper Celebration of Women in Computing in Bangalore, India, 2014.

Google and Facebook encourage their employees to spend a certain amount of their work days "inventing," which promotes the idea of creating new products.

Hackathons are tremendous opportunities for both novice and expert software engineers. They give new software engineers a chance to work with team members on a project and be able to add something to their résumés. All engineers, regardless of how long they've been in the business, can also benefit from hackathons by utilizing them as networking opportunities. Susan Chin, software engineer and first-place winner of the 2015 Emirates Travel Hackathon in San Francisco, was quoted in an article on PowertoFly.com about the best way to utilize hackathons for networking. She suggests seeking out the contact information of anyone who knows more than you and asking if you can stay in touch to ask more questions. This is a phenomenal way to build relationships at the same time that you're building a new product.

to code and then turned around and designed a course together for the site. After positive feedback from the site's users, the duo designed another course. And now, because of their ability to code and enjoyment of software engineering, they both work as part-time freelance web developers, while still finishing their homeschool education requirements. Khan Academy is another free site that teaches coding. It provides various tutorials, college and test-prep resources, and activities that correlate to STEAM activities for K-12. Google Education, Scratch, Try Objective-C, Free Code Camp, and Code Combat (which is designed like a video game) are other examples of free online resources to consider for code education.

Coding camps, or coding boot camps as they are also called, are another way to learn the ropes of software engineering. These intense courses generally crunch classes into a tight time frame, like two-to-three months. Some require up to 10 hours of class time per week, with an additional 20 to 30 hours of homework time. In coding camps, you often get one-on-one mentorship, which is a definite plus when it comes to learning difficult concepts and languages. Some of these camps are free, but others will definitely cost you. The fees can range anywhere from several thousand dollars to a percentage of your first year's salary (if you find a job after graduating from the camp). Experts argue that if aspiring software engineers decide on attending a coding camp, especially one that charges tuition, they should spend some time getting basic skills under their belt first and then use

Learning to code is free during the HTML500, an annual coding camp in Vancouver, Canada, where top tech companies teach attendees their tricks of the trade.

the camp as a way to take their repertoire to the next level.

Software engineer Paul DeVe suggests that people interested in software engineering really need to figure out first if they like solving software-related problems before they embark on the career. After all, there's no point investing time and money into something if you really don't like doing it. "Code.org is a fantastic website focused on teaching people of all ages how to code and how to solve problems with software," he explains. He also suggests trying out different technologies and seeing which one most interests you. "If you like websites and are curious about how to write responsive pages that do cool things, check out ReactJs or AngularJs. They're both free frameworks that make it really easy to quickly make cool web pages." He reminds us that "they may be antiquated by

Interview with a Software Engineer: Craig Boren

Why did you decide to become a software engineer?

Ever since my early teenage years, I always had a keen interest in technology, particularly with computers. Funny enough, this stemmed from my love for video games, which inherently led me to learn how those games were made, which of course opened my eyes to the really strange new world of computer code. Since then, I dabbled off and on, tinkering with and learning about the inner workings of computer code. However, upon entering college, I became somewhat disinterested in pursuing a degree in computer science primarily due to the fact that most of the curriculum dealt with theory (i.e., control structures, objects, functions, etc.) rather than the practicality and hands-on learning I desired. It wasn't until a few years after I had graduated from college that my career path took a turn into web design/development and eventually into more foundational web software engineering. It was at that point that my earlier training and interest in coding paid off and gave me the tools and skills to be successful.

What are the pros/cons of this career?

Just as with any career, there are both pros and cons in a career as a software engineer.

First, the pros: telecommuting allows for a flexible (work-from-home) schedule, good work/life balance, relatively low-stress environment, very generous pay and benefits, getting to work with highly intelligent, interesting people, challenging and highly satisfactory projects, and job security.

Cons: sometimes (rarely) required to work on weekends, technical tools are constantly evolving thus requiring incorporating new technologies and/or methodologies, and working on very important systems which can break and need debugging.

the time you graduate, but the concepts will remain the same." DeVe also suggests that "if you think databases might be your thing, start reading up on NoSQL and document databases. As it turns out, we've found much more efficient ways to store and access data in the last five years. Again, the particular technologies may go away, but the concepts will still be there, and your head start is going to make you look like a genius when it comes time to interview for your first job."

CHAPTER FOUR

Finding a Job

"Now is a fantastic time to be a software engineer." Expanding on this, software engineer Paul DeVe says, "Jobs are incredibly plentiful, and annual salaries put a person comfortably in the middle class. In bigger cities, larger companies actually have to fight to get new employees, meaning that a software engineer looking for a new job can be very picky about the type of work they accept and how much they are paid for it."

Even though the job outlook is great, that doesn't mean you can just sit back in your house and the job offers will just flow through your windows and doors on a summer breeze! You still need to do some legwork, including networking, in order to get your name out there, especially if you're new to the business. There are many suggestions on how best to do this. Here are some of them.

ATTEND CAREER AND JOB FAIRS

Career and job fairs are often held at local universities. They can be helpful networking resources for recent college grads and for people who are aiming for a mid-level career change. The best thing to remember about career fairs, though, is that they are only as good as you make them. Some people find job fairs pointless, and others find them useful. It depends on a variety of factors, but part of it is that you need to do your own preparation to make sure it's a success. First, you should research the fair and make sure the companies you are interested in will actually be there. Second, make sure you have researched those companies so you can be informed when talking to the recruiters. Third, dress professionally, bring plenty

Students have come prepared to this career fair at San Francisco State University. Bring along résumés, samples, and business cards so you can network with potential employers.

of copies of your résumé, and take time at each booth to properly network.

One job seeker in Israel, Jacob Share, had a poor experience at the first career fair he attended in Tel Aviv. However, after the experience, he realized that he was partly to blame because he hadn't properly prepared. In an article on JobMob, he explained some of the benefits that he has since discovered by going to other career fairs: they give people a chance to network, discover the latest job market trends, meet their competition, compare companies, get résumé help, and even take workshops offered by career coaches.

Create a Knock-Out Portfolio

As a software engineer, your portfolio is your best form of advertising—next to your in-person self, of course! Portfolios should tell prospective employers the following details: who you are, what kind of work you do, how you do that type of work, your goals for the future, and the type of projects and companies you'd like to work with. You should think of your portfolio as your personal brand.

Even if you're new to the industry, you can still create a knock-out website. Be sure to include all of your educational experiences. These include any projects you worked on in college, certifications you have earned, online courses you took, etc. Some online courses offer skill badges, similar to the merit badges given out in scouting programs. These badges show your competency in a variety of technical skills, languages, and so forth. Be sure to include every single software-related project you have ever completed. Show the process, not just the end result, and include both screenshots and expository text. Tell what you learned, what obstacles you overcame throughout the course of the project, and how you would improve it if you were to do it again. Another idea is to take a well-known website and completely redesign it to improve it. Also, ask any client, professor, or associate to write a testimonial for you. You can include these under a specified tab in the portfolio. Under a separate tab titled "Community Involvement," list out any groups, clubs, or organizations that you belong to. Also list out any hack-athons that you have participated in and what projects you created during that time.

TOP TIPS FOR SOFTWARE ENGINEERING INTERVIEWS

Software engineer Nathan Ekstrom is of the opinion that "most [job] interviewers want to get an idea of how you problem-solve, interact with people, and what you've done in the past." The overall goal is to see if you'll be a good fit for the company and if you know your stuff: "You will usually interview with a manager and one or more of the higher-level engineers who you would be working

The future is now. Technology jobs allow you to help create a new future.

with. They will most likely ask you how you would solve a simple problem, and you will end up writing code up on a whiteboard."

His number-one advice for interview success is to show confidence and don't rush in answering questions. "It is better to be correct than to be quick," he explains. He also advises to be straightforward in your questions. "If you don't know the answer to a question, just say so," he advises. "Trying to sound like you know something that you don't makes you end up sounding stupid."

Here are three more tips for interview success:

1. Be very familiar with basic data structure and algorithms. Essentially, this is like saying that a doctor who wants to find a job should have an expert knowledge of human anatomy. Basic data

structure and algorithms are the most fundamental parts of software engineering. Any candidate for a job in this industry who doesn't have a good foundation in these will not do well on a technical interview. Places like MyCodeSchool (a YouTube topic on the "Strong Programming Foundations" channel) offer some great free videos to help software engineers brush up on these topics.

2. Practice coding with the same materials that you will have in the interview. Some companies will have you code on a whiteboard. Some will have you use a computer. You'll want to practice at home with the same materials that you will use in the interview so you will feel the most comfortable in the setting and be able to do your best. As one expert notes, "In real life, if you want to swim the English Channel, would you limit your practice to laps at the local swimming pool? No, you would go test out the ocean waves, the salt water. Do the same here [as you prepare for your interview]." In order to do this, it is advisable to ask your point of contact what type of interview format the company will be using so you can prepare ahead of time.
3. Chill out. Realize that you'll likely make some mistakes in the interview process. That is normal, so don't think it's the end of the world if things don't go exactly as you'd like them to. One of the key points of software engineering is that rarely do things go

exactly as you'd like them to. That's what coding, testing, recoding, and retesting is all about. So if you can show that you are adaptable and can stay calm under pressure despite the presence of problems, you'll have a better shot of landing the job.

Interview with a Software Engineer: Amber Elstad

Why did you decide to become a software engineer?

Programming is just what made sense to me, even as a kid. I wasn't exactly sure what I was going to do when I graduated college, but I found myself in a programming position and that's where I've basically stayed. Not so much the same company, but similar roles.

What education/training did you need to have?

I do have a BS in computer science. Many of my classes, not just the programming language specific ones, laid the foundation for me to learn what I needed to know when I would start a job. Knowing the basics of a few different languages made me flexible in picking up new languages as the job required it.

What is a typical work day like for you as a software engineer?

Right now our focus is primarily customer-facing defect corrections, but soon we'll be back to incorporating new development into the mix. We have a daily standup in the morning; talk about cases we are working on, since it's possible that another on the team might have insight or time to help out; also address what our estimated work will be. Then I answer emails, review open cases, contact clients as necessary, and determine next steps for my open cases. Depending on the cause of the issue, I may have to write a data fix or test/step through code to see where an issue was happening. If it's a code issue I can fix, then I write up a work item describing what the client saw, the steps to recreate it, and acceptance criteria that will help identify when testing is complete. Once the code change is made and tested on my machine, it gets sent off for a code review by my team. Any back and forth due to comments on the code review is resolved and then it gets checked in and sent to QA. Then, once all the work that can be done on my current cases is done, I look at the queue for my team and pick up the next item on the list. Throughout the day, I check to see if there are any outstanding code reviews from my team that I can go over.

NETWORK, NETWORK, NETWORK

According to the experts at Monster.com, networking is an "essential part of any successful job search." There are a variety of ways to network: both in person and through online resources. In-person networking opportunities include those found in college settings, internships, workshops, hackathons, seminars, classes, meetups, clients, and so forth. Essentially, as a software engineer, the more you can get out there, meet, and work with other engineers and IT professionals, the broader the professional network you'll be able to build. Monster.com also recommends adding non-IT people to your network as well, which makes perfect sense. Associating with people in a variety of contexts is beneficial for job searching because you never know who may have great job leads for you among the people they know. Spread your networking net far and wide to include people you know from your church, community clubs, hobby groups, volunteer organizations, neighbors, health clubs, political groups, the PTA, and so forth.

Nathan Ekstrom recommends utilizing a variety of approaches when it comes to networking for job searches:

> *A lot of times, doing a paid summer internship for a company means you will have a job with them when you graduate, so I would recommend them. Most metropolitan areas and schools have job fairs, programming events, or contests. Find out when they are, and attend or compete. It is also a good idea to find an open-source project that is doing something you find interesting and start contributing. Being able to point a potential employer to code you've written is a big plus.*

Social media is not only a great way to stay in contact with your in-person network, but also a great way to branch out and add more "friends" to your network. More sites like this are certainly going to be added in the future, but for the present moment places like Facebook, LinkedIn, Twitter, Xing, Google+, Pinterest, Vine, Meet-up, and Instagram are all great social media resources. Rebecca White, director of a staffing firm, stated in an article on *Business News Daily* that it is crucial for job seekers to utilize social media: "Not only does this show that they are current on the latest technologies, but it also provides them [with a way] to stay in touch with their colleagues, expand their professional network, and open themselves up to other career opportunities."

An article from *Entrepreneur* expands the significance of social media as a networking tool: "In the past five years, connecting on social networking sites has rocketed from a niche activity into a phenomenon that engages tens of millions of internet users." The article discusses the ways to best utilize the internet for networking purposes. One is by connecting with high-level networkers (HLNs), people who have "at least 500 connections and powerful profiles." These people are fantastic to connect with because if you have a particular need, they have a broader base to reach out to. Join groups related to your profession and take an active part in them, or find industry-related blogs to follow.

However, a word of caution must be issued when it comes to using social media for your job searches. Be extra careful to keep your own sites (including your personal ones) as professional as possible. If you think it doesn't

Networking online is crucial for success. Set up an online professional profile such as this one at http://www.linkedin.com and keep it up to date.

matter to a job search that you post party pictures, extreme viewpoints, or other related material, then you're wrong. Nicola McGuane, a consultant at recruitment firm Morgan McKinley, was quoted in an article on this topic for the *Guardian*. She said, "The world has become a much smaller place and you never know who your future boss is connected to, allowing them to see your activities." This concept doesn't just apply to when you're hunting for a job, either. It also applies during your employment. It's never a good idea to post negative comments about your boss online, especially if you are connected with anyone associated with the workplace. It's also incredibly unwise to post pics of you kicking back and relaxing on the job when you should be working. People have been known to get fired for these kinds of activities, so just keep that in mind. Just be smart about your posting choices so things won't come back to haunt you later on.

CHAPTER FIVE

Always Learning

Once you have a job as a software engineer, it isn't just a lifetime of smooth sailing where you can kick back, relax, and collect a fat paycheck without any need for continuing education. Jobs in IT require constant learning, and that's because IT is constantly changing. If you don't keep up on all of the recent trends in the industry, you will soon be left in the dust. The endlessly changing nature of IT might be a deterrent for some people, but for others, it's actually one of the things that attracted them to the industry in the first place. One developer explained it this way: "I love IT because every day I learn something that I didn't know the day before."

Using the Internet

One way, and perhaps the best way, to stay current on new trends in IT is to utilize online resources.

Listening to professional audiobooks or podcasts while commuting is a great way to stay updated in the IT world.

There are podcasts, YouTube videos, and instructional websites that can help inform you on all kinds of topics related to information technology. Podcasts can help inform you about industry news—and the great part is that they provide opportunities for multitasking, since they can be listened to while you're doing other things like exercising, cooking, cleaning, or commuting to work. YouTube videos can be found on all kinds of IT topics as well. You can search out different interviews, seminars, and workshops presented by industry professionals. You can find instructional videos that teach new languages, coding techniques, and ways to address various software-related issues. In addition, the internet offers many instructional websites, as was described in the previous chapter, that provide classes on all kinds of topics in the software engineering field. Following people on Twitter is also a great way to further your education online and stay up-to-date on the latest technologies. By searching for specific topics on Twitter and following people who specialize in those topics, the computer will "learn" that this is of interest to you and will start filling your feed with related tweets.

ATTENDING MEETUPS, SEMINARS, AND SIMILAR EVENTS

In-person events are not just great for networking, they're also fantastic resources for furthering education and adding up-to-date training to your résumé. Meetup is a site that allows people to search for groups on various topics. At the writing of this book, there were 821 Meetup groups related to software engineering around the world with more than 311,820 members. Related topics in these groups included software development, computer programming, web development, programming languages, mobile development, and software architecture. One particular group with nearly 7,000 members is BASE: Bay Area Software Engineers. It hosts software-related events in the San Francisco Bay Area and provides people from all different backgrounds a chance to meet, learn, and network.

Top Schools for Computer Engineering

Every year, the *US News & World Report* publishes its "best of" lists in various categories for universities and colleges around the United States. Here are the top ten computer engineering programs in the country for undergraduate students as of 2016.

Ranking for Computer Engineering Programs in the United States:

1. Massachusetts Institute of Technology (MIT), Cambridge, MA
2. Stanford University, Stanford, CA
3. University of California–Berkeley, Berkeley, CA
4. University of Illinois–Urbana-Champaign, Urbana, IL
5. Carnegie Mellon University, Pittsburgh, PA
6. Georgia Institute of Technology, Atlanta, GA
7. University of Texas–Austin, Austin, TX
8. University of Michigan–Ann Arbor, Ann Arbor, MI
9. California Institute of Technology, Pasadena, CA
10. Cornell University, Ithaca, NY

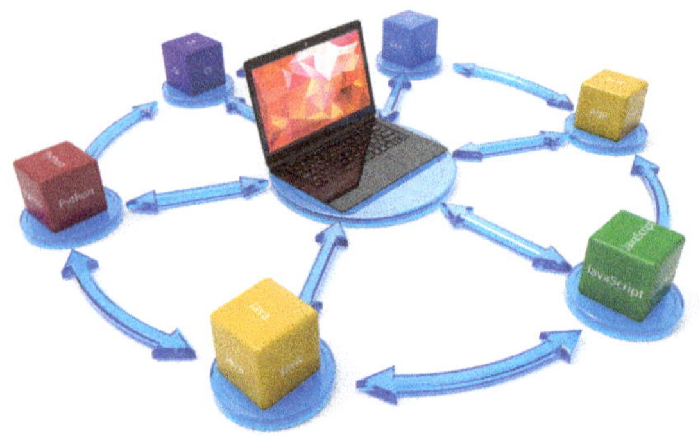

Learning new computer languages helps you stay marketable in an ever-changing industry.

LOOKING FOR ADVANCEMENT OPPORTUNITIES

There are many ways that a software engineer can advance in the industry. "The company I work for has six different career levels for web developers, each with a higher pay grade than the previous level," Craig Boren explains. Advancing your skills, learning the latest and greatest technologies, picking up a new language, and pursuing your own projects are all ways to advance in the business. Nathan Ekstrom advises that to stay marketable, software engineers should "learn multiple programming languages. Each language you learn increases your understanding of basic programming principles and makes you more valuable." He emphasized that programmers don't just use one language—they use many of them. "The important part of programming is to learn the fundamentals," he said, "Once you really understand those, you can map them onto any language."

Another way to advance your career and make yourself more marketable is by specializing. "I'm a front-end developer who specialized in web-based, single-page applications, which mostly means that I can make fancy websites that do cool stuff," Paul DeVe explains in an interview. "This absolutely makes me marketable when looking for a position. The great thing though is that with how much software has invaded every part of our lives, the variety of software engineering jobs has increased. Finding an aspect of software that interests a person and getting good at it will make that person marketable. A person can focus on the layout and styling of web pages,

Interview with a Software Engineer: Paul DeVe

Why did you decide to become a software engineer?

Really, it was two things. First, I blame my dad. When I was around seven, my dad brought home a Commodore 64 from his school. It was the coolest thing I'd ever seen in my entire life (as much of it as I'd lived so far), and I was instantly hooked. Mostly it was for the video games, but as the years went on, I actually got to be pretty proficient in the rest of it. My dad would drive us from Modesto, CA, to San Francisco so that we could go to computer swap meets. He helped me build my first computer. If not for my dad encouraging me and helping me explore something that I loved, I'm not sure where I'd be today.

But loving computers isn't enough to be a successful software engineer. With all the time I'd spent with computer software, I still went off to college thinking that I'd be an electrical engineer. The physical construction fascinated me, and I couldn't wait to find out more. It wasn't until I took my first electrical engineering course that I learned that no matter how much I was interested in how circuits work, it didn't mean that I was going to enjoy solving those types of problems. It also reminded me of how much fun I DID have solving software problems. Looking back, I count myself very lucky to have already found something I was interested in. It just took seeing my other options to convince me that I'd picked right the first time.

Did you take any classes in high school to prepare you for (or get you interested in) this career?

I did, but I had to make the class myself. When I was graduating from high school in 1995, the internet was brand new and schools hadn't realized quite how much computers were going to change our lives. In my senior year, a few of us with some time to spare got a faculty sponsor and created our own programming class. By the time I went to college, I was definitely ahead of the curve.

Playing games on the Commodore 64 meant learning to use a joystick, rather than the modern mouse or touchscreen you'd be more familiar with on today's computer.

something that is surprisingly complex and infuriating given that so many browsers work differently. A person can focus on data storage and access in order to persist the ridiculous amount of data that we now capture and use on a daily basis. The list goes on, but the point is that there are a lot of different marketable options."

EXCITING CAREER WITH MANY POSSIBILITIES

Information technology, especially software engineering, is an exciting field with many possibilities. Because the software engineering field is in high demand with a growing job market and fewer workers than the market demands, the field generally offers very generous compensation packages. From an altruistic perspective, though, software engineering is an attractive career choice because it offers professionals a chance to create products that have a real tangible impact on people's lives. Jananda Hill, a software engineer at Northrup Grumman who works on the software for space satellites, was asked in an interview on Engineergirl.org what she liked the most about her career. Her answer summed up the general consensus of how many people who have chosen to spend their careers designing, writing, creating, and testing software also feel. She said, "I love the creativity that's involved, and the satisfaction that comes when you actually make something work."

GLOSSARY

ANDROID An operating system that is used on non-iOS based mobile devices.

C A computer language derived from an earlier language named "B." It was developed in 1969 by Dennis Richie at the Bell Laboratories. It is a Unix operating system. LINUX is based on the C program.

C++ A computer language that is a modified version of C. It was created by Bjarne Stroustrup in 1983 and is considered one of the top ten programming languages, and possibly the most popular language in existence.

CENTRAL PROCESSING UNIT The physical part of a computer that processes the information and instructions that are brought into the computer.

COBOL This is an acronym for Common Business Oriented Language. It is a computer language invented by Dr. Grace Hopper in 1959. It is still used in business, banking, hospital, government, automotive, traffic signal systems, and the US Post Office.

IOS An operating system used specifically on Apple -based mobile devices.

JAVA A computer programming language developed by James Gosling in 1995. It was originally created to run interactive television. Now it is used by billions of personal computers around the world, and many websites are unable to work properly without it.

JAVASCRIPT A computer programming language, originally called Mocha. It was developed by Brendan Eich of Netscape in 1995. It uses language that is similar to C and is not related to Java. It's used by browsers, used to control web pages, and on mobile apps.

OBJECTIVE-C A computer language that is a subset of the C language. It is used to create software for Apple products or the iOS system.

PHP This is an acronym for Personal Home Page, or PHP: Hypertext Preprocessor. This is a computer language designed by Rasmus Lerdof in 1995. It was developed to replace Perl scripts on Lerdof's personal web page. It is now an integral part of the web; millions of websites are written using PHP.

PROGRAMS A sequence of commands or operations—a set of steps that tell a machine to perform a certain function.

PUNCH CARDS An early method of data storage. Each card was punched into a code (either by hand or by machine) and then placed into a specific order to give instructions to the machine.

PYTHON A computer language named for Monty Python, a British comedy group popular in the 1960s-70s. It was developed by Guido Van Rossum in 1989 to fix problems in another language. It is now used by Google Search, YouTube, and NASA.

RUBY A computer language that is named for July's birthstone. It was created in 1993 by Yukihiro "Matz" Matsumoto by blending a variety of languages together. It can be used in web applications in conjunction with Rails.

STANDUP MEETING An informal meet that is usually held first thing in the morning. Attendees stand up during the meeting in order to encourage brevity.

SYSTEMS SOFTWARE Programs that run a computer's hardware and application programs; in other words, this is the "middle man" between the hardware and the actual user programs.

VACUUM TUBES A glass or metal tube that has its gas removed to form a vacuum. For a computer, these gasless tubes contain electrodes and are used to control the electron flow for the computer. Known as "valves" in Great Britain.

Association of Women in Computing

P.O. Box 2768
Oakland, CA 94602
Website: http://www.awc-hq.org/home.html
This organization was founded in 1978 in Washington, D.C. It is one of the first professional organizations focused solely on women in computing. Members include software engineers, system analysts, operators, technical writers, trainers, and consultants. The mission of the organization is to encourage women to enter the field of computing and help them advance once they choose this career. Networking opportunities through nationwide chapters is part of this organization's appeal.

Canada's Association of IT Professionals

5090 Explorer Drive, Suite 801
Mississauga, ON L4W 4T9
Canada
(905) 602-1370
Website: http://www.cips.ca
CIPS was founded in 1958 to establish standards in the IT industry in Canada. CIPS offers networking opportunities to its members, provides certification in ISP and ITCP designations and accreditation for IT programs, and serves as a voice to the Canadian government for issues related to the IT industry.

Canadian Women in Computing

176 Thorvaldson Building
110 Science Place
Saskatoon, SK S7N 5C9

Canada
(306) 966-2073
Website: http://acmw.usask.ca
The purpose of this organization is to provide information and support for Canadian women who have chosen careers in computing, or who want to do so. The organization hopes to improve the working and learning environments of women in the industry and encourage policy makers to help these goals become reality.

Codecademy
49 W 27th Street, 4th Floor
New York, NY 10001
Website: https://www.codecademy.com
This educational institution offers students a chance to learn coding in major programming languages, such as Python, PHP, JQuery, JavaScript, and Ruby. As of 2016, there were 24 million people using Codecademy around the world. Students include teens, college students, and professionals of all ages who are looking for career changes.

Code.org
1501 4th Avenue, Suite 900
Seattle, WA 98101
Website: https://code.org
This organization was founded in 2013. It is a non profit dedicated to the philosophy that "every student in every school should have the opportunity to learn computer science." Nearly half of the students who take Code.org courses are female students, unrepresented minorities, or students on

free or reduced meals at schools. Courses range from those geared toward elementary students, all the way through high school. Students learn all kinds of programming, including smartphone apps, games, websites, and more.

Computing Research Association

1828 L Street NW, Suite 800
Washington, D.C. 20036-4632
(202) 234-2111
Website: http://cra.org
CRA was founded in 1972 with a mission to "enhance innovation by joining with industry, government, and academia to strengthen research and advanced education in computing." The organization's membership includes more than 200 North American computer science organizations, laboratories, centers, and societies. CRA offers various resources to its members and holds annual events where members can network and consult with each other on various computer science topics.

Destination Imagination

1111 South Union Avenue
Cherry Hill, NJ 08002
(888) 321-1503
Website: https://www.destinationimagination.org
DI is a non profit educational organization that is led by volunteers and focused on project-based learning in STEM, arts, and social entrepreneurship. The purpose of the organization is to teach students the creative process and encourage them to become the next generation of leaders

and innovators. Students gain skills in creative and critical thinking, team building, problem solving, risk taking, project management, and perseverance, thereby attaining greater self-confidence through having those skills. More than 1.5 million students have benefitted from the programs offered by DI since 1999.

National Center for Women and Information Technology

University of Colorado
Campus Box 417 UCB
Boulder, CO 8309
(303) 735-6671
Website: https://www.ncwit.org
This non profit organization stretches across 700 universities, companies, nonprofits, and government organizations around the United States. The organization's mission is to encourage more girls (K-12) and women to pursue careers in information technology. It uses a three-pronged strategy to achieve this mission: forming alliances, providing free research-based resources, and offering educational programs.

WEBSITES

Because of the changing nature of internet links, Rosen Publishing has developed an online list of websites related to the subject of this book. This site is updated regularly. Please use this link to access the list:

http://www.rosenlinks.com/TECHT/software

For Further Reading

Abraham, Nikhil. *Coding for Dummies*. Hoboken, NJ: John Wiley & Sons, Inc., 2015.

Duggan, Michael. *iPad Action Gaming for Teens*. Boston, MA: Cengage Learning, 2014.

Feiler, Jesse. *iOS App Development for Dummies*. Hoboken, NJ: John Wiley & Sons, Inc., 2014.

Ford, Jerry Lee, Jr. *Scratch 2.0 Programming for Teens*. Boston, MA: Cengage Learning, 2014.

Johnson, Dean R., and Carol A. Palmer. *5 Steps to a 5 AP Computer Science A 2017 Edition*. New York: McGraw-Hill Education, 2016.

Lambert, Kenneth A. *Python Programming for Teens*. Boston, MA: Cengage Learning, 2015.

McGrath, Mike. *Coding for Beginners in Easy Steps: Basic Programming for All Ages*. Warwickshire, UK: Easy Steps Limited, 2015.

Mueller, John Paul, and Luca Massaron. *Python for Data Science for Dummies*. Hoboken, NJ: John Wiley & Sons, Inc., 2015.

Sande, Warren, and Carter Sande. *Computer Programming for Kids and Other Beginners*. Shelter Island, NY: Manning Publications Co., 2014.

Sommerville, Ian. *Software Engineering (10th Edition)*. Harlow, England: Pearson Education, 2016.

Stephens, Rod. *Beginning Software Engineering*. Indianapolis, IN: John Wiley & Sons, Inc., 2015.

BIBLIOGRAPHY

Allred, Casey. Personal interview with the author, September 2016.

"Best Technology Jobs: Number 2, Software Engineers." *US News & World Report*. Retrieved October 9, 2016. http://money.usnews.com/careers/best-jobs/software-developer.

Boren, Craig. Personal interview with the author, September 2016.

Brewer, Kristie. "What Your Social Media Presence Says About You." TheGuardian.com, April 20, 2016. https://jobs.theguardian.com/article/what-your-social-media-presence-says-about-you.

Bureau of Labor Statistics. "Software Developers." *Occupational Outlook Handbook*, December 17, 2015. http://www.bls.gov/ooh/computer-and-information-technology/software-developers.htm#tab-6.

Cirincione, Mary. "Teen Apps Developer Sets Sights on Future as Next Steve Jobs." *US News & World Report*, May 12, 2015. http://www.usnews.com/news/the-next-generation-of-stem/articles/2015/05/12/teen-app-developer-sets-sights-on-future-as-next-steve-jobs.

Codecademy. "Codecademy Stories: Joah Gerstenberg and Halley Higgins." Retrieved October 9, 2016. https://www.codecademy.com/stories/91.

Collier, Bruce. "The Little Engines That Could've: The Calculating Machines of Charles Babbage." PhD diss., Harvard University, 1970. http://robroy.dyndns.info/collier.

ComputerHistory. "The Babbage Engine, A Brief History." Retrieved October 7, 2016. http://www.computerhistory.org

/babbage/history.

Curtis, Sophie. "Colossus at 70: The Computer That Helped Bring down Hitler." *Telegraph*, February 5, 2014. http://www.telegraph.co.uk/technology/news/10618866/Colossus-at-70-the-computer-that-helped-bring-down-Hitler.html.

DeVe, Paul. Personal interview with the author, October 9, 2016.

DrKitVideos. "Advice from a Computer Science, Software Engineering (BS) Student from drkit.org." YouTube Video, 4:38. Posted April 28, 2013. https://www.youtube.com/watch?v=azvF_nBoR7I.

Ekstrom, Nathan. Personal interview with the author, October 10, 2016.

Elstad, Amber. Personal interview with the author, September 2016.

Entrepreneur. "The Right Way to Network on Social Media." February 19, 2015. https://www.entrepreneur.com/article/241959.

Gausepohl, Shannon. "Social Media Success: A Guide for Job Seekers." *Business News Daily*, June 17, 2016. http://www.businessnewsdaily.com/7728-social-media-job-seeker-guide.html#sthash.c8RzEcDJ.dpuf.

Hayworth, Roy. Personal interview with the author, September 2016.

"Jananda Hill." Engineergirl. Retrieved October 10, 2016. http://www.engineergirl.org/Engineers/Directory/2971.aspx.

Jaynes, Justin. Personal interview with the author, September 2016.

Kelley, Megan. "Four Reasons Every Female Developer Should Attend a Hackathon," PowertoFly.com, May 18, 2016. https://connect.powertofly.com/four-reasons-every-female-developer-should-attend-a-hackathon-1805441076.html.

Morgan, Elle. "A Day in the Life: Front End Engineer." YouTube Video, 1:49. Posted December 9, 2011. https://www.youtube.com/watch?v=w9UDoIeOG-E.

MyCodeSchool. "MyCodeSchool.com – Walk-through and Getting Started." YouTube Video, 2:30. Posted September 6, 2013. https://www.youtube.com/watch?v=g7ORxNolZOM.

Nelson, Jeremy. Personal interview with the author, September 2016.

"Sayari Ghosh." Engineergirl. Retrieved October 7, 2016. http://www.engineergirl.org/Engineers/Directory/19971.aspx.

Share, Jacob. "25 Reasons Job Fairs Are Not a Ridiculous Waste of Time." JobMob. Retrieved October 10, 2016. https://jobmob.co.il/blog/job-fairs-reasons-to-go.

Truong, Kevin. "Day in the life of a Game Developer." YouTube Video, 1:19. Posted May 26, 2012. https://www.youtube.com/watch?v=YrYs_9lEGyY.

"Undergraduate Computer Engineering Rankings." *US News & World Report*. Retrieved October 5, 2016. http://colleges.usnews.rankingsandreviews.com/best-colleges/search?school-type=engineering-doctorate&ranking=computer&_mode=list.

INDEX

W

X

Y